Community Helpers

Helping with Sports and Games

by Trudy Becker

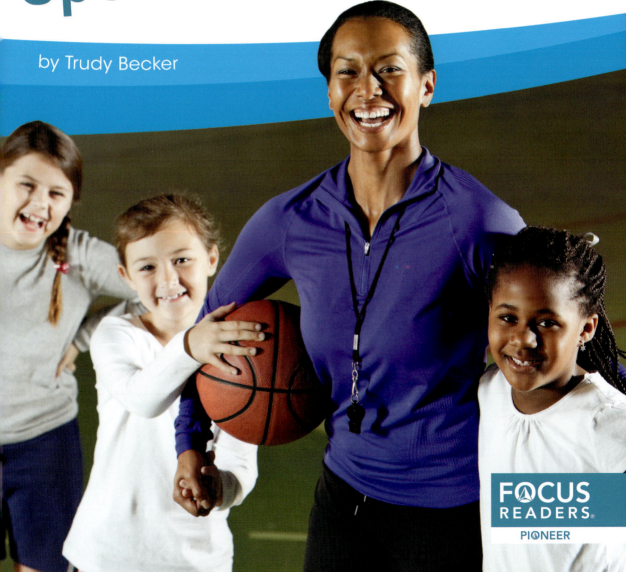

www.focusreaders.com

Copyright © 2024 by Focus Readers®, Mendota Heights, MN 55120. All rights reserved. No part of this book may be reproduced or utilized in any form or by any means without written permission from the publisher.

Focus Readers is distributed by North Star Editions:
sales@northstareditions.com | 888-417-0195

Produced for Focus Readers by Red Line Editorial.

Photographs ©: iStockphoto, cover, 1, 7, 11; Shutterstock Images, 4, 8, 12, 15, 17, 18, 21

Library of Congress Cataloging-in-Publication Data
Library of Congress Cataloging-in-Publication Data is available on the Library of Congress website.

ISBN
979-8-88998-021-6 (hardcover)
979-8-88998-064-3 (paperback)
979-8-88998-148-0 (ebook pdf)
979-8-88998-107-7 (hosted ebook)

Printed in the United States of America
Mankato, MN
012024

About the Author

Trudy Becker lives in Minneapolis, Minnesota. She likes exploring new places and loves anything involving books.

Table of Contents

CHAPTER 1
A Coach's Words 5

CHAPTER 2
Coaching Kids 9

CHAPTER 3
Helping at Games 13

THAT'S AMAZING!
Referees 16

CHAPTER 4
Other Ways to Help 19

Focus on Helping with Sports and Games • 22
Glossary • 23
To Learn More • 24
Index • 24

Chapter 1

A Coach's Words

A whistle blows. It is halftime. The soccer team runs off the field. They gather around their coach. They listen carefully to her words.

Soon, the second half starts. The team plays hard. They win! The coach feels proud. Coaching is not her job. She is a **volunteer**. She does it to help her **community**.

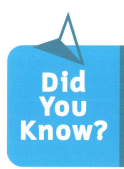

Did You Know? Sports are a great way to be **social**. They help bring people together.

Chapter 2

Coaching Kids

Many communities have sports teams for kids. These teams need lots of helpers. Coaches are one example. Coaches lead the teams.

Most coaches have played the sport before. They know a lot about it. So, they can help kids get better. They can help their teams have fun, too.

Did You Know? School teams also have coaches. But those coaches are often paid.

Chapter 3

Helping at Games

Games often need other kinds of helpers, too. Some volunteers sell tickets. They collect money and help people enter the games.

Many people enjoy snacks while watching games. So, some volunteers work in **concession stands**. They help sell food and drinks.

Did You Know? Some volunteers work as **mascots**. They cheer and wear fun costumes.

THAT'S AMAZING!

Referees

Many sports need referees. These people make sure players follow the rules. This role is sometimes a job. People get paid to do it. But other times, volunteers do it. They might love the sport. Or they might want to support nearby **leagues**.

Chapter 4

Other Ways to Help

People can help with sports in other ways, too. Sports teams need lots of **supplies**. People can **donate** money or items. Teams can use those items to play.

People can also help at the fields or courts. Some helpers cut the grass. Some set up goals and supplies. Others clean up after games. All these helpers make games possible.

Did You Know? Sometimes big sports events come to town. The events often need extra helpers.

FOCUS ON
Helping with Sports and Games

Write your answers on a separate piece of paper.

1. Write a few sentences that explain the main idea of Chapter 4.

2. Would you want to be a coach? Why or why not?

3. Who makes sure that players follow the rules?
    - A. volunteer
    - B. coach
    - C. referee

4. Why would donating money help teams?
    - A. Teams only play if they earn money.
    - B. Teams could use it to buy supplies.
    - C. Teams always need to pay coaches.

Answer key on page 24.

Glossary

community
A group of people and the places where they spend time.

concession stands
Stalls where people buy food and drinks at events.

donate
To give something away to people in need.

leagues
Groups of teams that play against one another.

mascots
Characters that represent sports teams.

social
Being around other people.

supplies
Items that people need to do something.

volunteer
A person who helps without being paid.

To Learn More

BOOKS

Adamson, Thomas K. *Basketball*. Minneapolis: Bellwether Media, 2020.

Downs, Kieran. *Softball*. Minneapolis: Bellwether Media, 2021.

NOTE TO EDUCATORS

Visit **www.focusreaders.com** to find lesson plans, activities, links, and other resources related to this title.

Index

C
coach, 5–6, 9–10

R
referees, 16

S
supplies, 19–20

T
tickets, 13

Answer Key: 1. Answers will vary; 2. Answers will vary; 3. C; 4. B